LET'S PLAY SPORTS!

# SWIMMING

by Tessa Kenan



## TABLE OF CONTENTS

tadpole books

# WORDS TO KNOW

dives

floats

jump

kicks

pool

swims

# LET'S SWIM!

Let's go to the pool!

We wear swimsuits.

We jump in!

He dives in!

He kicks.

**She swims.**

He floats.

Let's swim!

# LET'S REVIEW!

**What is this swimmer doing?**

# INDEX